ER 43 N 300

THE SPIRIT OF

SOMERSET

CHRISTOPHER NICHOLSON

HALSGROVE

First published in Great Britain in 2008

British Library Cataloguing-in-Publication Data
A CIP record for this title is available from the British Library

ISBN 978 1 84114 596 9

HALSGROVE
Halsgrove House
Ryelands Industrial Estate
Bagley Road, Wellington
Somerset TA21 9PZ
Tel: 01823 653777
Fax: 01823 216796
email: sales@halsgrove.com
website: www.halsgrove.com

Printed and bound by D'Auria Industrie Grafiche Spa, Italy

Introduction

Somerset – 'Land of the Summer People' is its ancient meaning. The same could be true today as Somerset continues to attract a huge influx of summer visitors. Why do they come? Most because of its natural beauty that they can walk, drive or cycle through. Somerset has such a diverse range of scenery that finding something of interest is not difficult for the visitor; golden beaches, rocky cliffs, wild moorland, rolling hills, and flat marshlands – Somerset has them all.

It's also a wonderful place for a photographer to live. Panoramic landscapes, big skies, ever-changing seascapes, historical architecture, grand houses, thatched cottages and natural history are just some of the subjects to point a camera at. It has been an impossible task to cover every corner or aspect of life in the county within this modest volume so I've tried to choose photographs that show the kind of places or views that keep people returning to the Land of the Summer People year after year. If you live in Somerset, or know it well, I hope you will find something of interest as you turn these pages.

Chris Nicholson

Victorian elegance
The minimalist Victorian elegance
of the recently restored Clevedon Pier
attracts many visitors. Beyond is
the coast of Wales.

Opposite page:
Weston super Mare
Exactly how far the tide recedes
at low water can be clearly seen from the
summit of Brean Down – so too can
Weston's original pier on Birnbeck Island.

The tide turns
When the sea returns the boats moored in front of the old Knightstone
Theatre bob back to life. On the horizon is the rounded hump of Steep Holm.

Bucket and spade holidays

Weston is very much a 'traditional' seaside resort, one of its many attractions being donkey rides on the beach. Every possible item of beach paraphernalia is available from Weston's well stocked beach stalls.

Waiting for the visitors to return

In winter the once-bustling beach attracts only dog walkers and horse riders. The Grand Pier was built in 1933 and still retains much of its art-deco styling.

Opposite page:
Century-old wreck

This is all that remains of the *SS Nornan*, driven ashore by a south-westerly gale during March 1897. It's now a tourist attraction known as the 'Berrow Wreck'.

A lighthouse on stilts
Burnham-on-Sea's unusual wooden-legged lighthouse guides vessels safely into the mouth of the River Parrett and on to Bridgwater.

Opposite page:
Blue Anchor wheat
At Blue Anchor Bay the wheat fields extend to the very edge of the cliffs. Across the bay lie Dunster and Minehead.

Where woodland meets the sea

Minehead is another Victorian seaside resort with a harbour
set against a backdrop of picturesque wooded cliffs.

High tide at Porlock

Porlock Weir is a particularly attractive tidal creek nestling under the wooded slopes of Exmoor and the home berth for a small number of yachts and boats.

The Somerset Levels

The Levels are acres of flat land, once flooded but now drained by miles
of rhynes lined with countless willow trees that cover large tracts of central Somerset.
In this view we are looking across part of the Levels towards the Mendip hills.

Opposite page:
Drifting

The Levels are the home to huge numbers of swans – like these two and
their cygnet drifting along the Cripps River on a winter's afternoon.

Winter floods

During really wet winters the rhynes can't cope and the fields themselves flood – sometimes to a depth of several feet.

Opposite page:
Dawn reflection

Early morning on the Levels. The winter flooding has created a perfect reflection of the willow tree in the Cripps River.

Island refuge

Rising out of the Levels there are several 'islands' of resistant rocks like this
one at Burrow Mump. The ruined church on the top dates from 1793.

Opposite page:
Winter wonderland

Snow doesn't come very often to the Levels, but when it does it can be magical.

Misty dawn

Winter sometimes brings early
morning mist that blankets the moors
until a weak sun can break through
with eerie results.

Opposite page:
Mendip walkers

A group of walkers descend from the
distinctively shaped Crook Peak at the
western end of Mendip. Beyond is
the circular reservoir at Cheddar.

Gorgeous!

Cheddar Gorge is Somerset's No.1 tourist attraction – and no wonder. The towering limestone cliffs are the remnants of a collapsed cave system from prehistoric times.

Opposite page: **Exmoor survivor**

There aren't many trees above a certain altitude on Exmoor and this is one of the few that has survived. Beyond are the rolling Brendon Hills.

Summer splendour
This view shows Dunkery Beacon from the north-west in high summer. The road that snakes its way up from Porlock is visible on the left.

Summit view
The top of Dunkery Beacon is the highest point in Somerset. It's marked by a cairn bearing a plaque commemorating its hand-over to the National Trust in 1935.

Quantock combe
The Quantock Hills are a mixture of open moorland and wooded valleys or 'combes'.
The myriad shades of green seen here are from the new season's leaf growth in May.

Cothelstone ponies
Wild ponies are a common sight on the Quantocks, particularly this group that live on
Cothelstone Hill near the group of trees on the summit known as the Seven Sisters.

Dunster market

At the top of the High Street in Dunster is the six-sided Yarn Market dating from
1609 when the village was an important cloth manufacturing centre.

Fortified Gatehouse

It has all the usual 'castle' architecture – turrets, towers and castellations – including this fortified gatehouse.

Opposite page: **Somerset fortress**

Dunster Castle dominates the village from its imposing site. When it was first built the Bristol Channel, in the distance, used to lap against the rock on which it stands.

Riverside variety
The buildings that line Bridgwater's West Quay – with their many different
architectural influences – are among the best features of the town.

Georgian elegance
Bridgwater's magnificent Georgian terrace on Castle Street was completed in 1730,
but to be able to admire it like this – without parked cars – is a rare sight indeed.

Chimneys and cobbles
Vicar's Close, Wells, still houses the clergy
of the Cathedral, and dates from the
middle of the fourteenth century. It is
the oldest street in Europe.

Opposite page:
Golden glory
It's the sheer beauty of the stonework on
the west front of Wells Cathedral that draws
thousands of visitors every year. It is best
viewed with a setting sun in late afternoon.

Shadows on the lawn
Taunton's Castle dates from 1138 and was
the focus of various activities during the
Wars of the Roses and the Civil War.

Opposite page:
Market day, Wells
A short walk through Penniless Porch leads to the
Market Square. Surrounded by elegant shops, it's
still the site of the colourful twice weekly market.

Market Cross

Somerton's Market Cross of 1673 bears an uncanny similarity with the Yarn Market at Dunster. Somerton is the epitome of a rural Somerset market town.

Opposite page:
Sunlight on the church

A shaft of sunlight picks out the village of Middlezoy – 'zoy' being an Norse word for 'island'. These were areas of higher ground that stood proud of the flooded Levels that surrounded them – thus making an excellent site for a settlement. The Polden Hills are in the distance.

Calendar favourite

The pack horse bridge at Allerford is a favourite view of calendar publishers – a reminder of the days when horses loaded with wool made their way on and off Exmoor.

Opposite page:
Chimneys and thatch

Tall chimneys and thatched roofs are characteristic of cottages in parts of West Somerset. This delightful example is in Bossington.

White church

Whitewashed churches are rare in Somerset. This unusual example is at Selworthy and enjoys stunning views across to Exmoor from its churchyard.

Opposite page:
Vivary Park and Barracks

Jellalabad Barracks – the former home of the Somerset Light Infantry – overlook the park and iron fountain erected in memory of Queen Victoria.

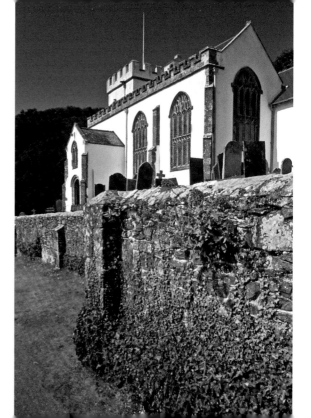

Herbaceous borders

The lawns and borders to the east of the house are absolutely stunning and are notable for the unusual shape of the gazebos in the corners.

Opposite page: **Magnificent mansion**

Montacute is probably the grandest of Somerset's grand houses. Built from honey-coloured ham stone in the last years of the sixteenth century and offered 'for scrap' in 1931 before being rescued by the National Trust.

Wallflowers in a Walled Garden

Barrington is surrounded by a number of individual
garden 'rooms' with different themes. This is
the stunning Pool Garden.

Opposite page:
Autumn shadows

Barrington Court is another magnificent sixteenth-century manor
house near Ilminster. On the left is Strode House – a later
addition but now converted to a restaurant and luxury flats.

Historic Hestercombe

Hestercombe House Gardens above Taunton surround the headquarters of the Somerset Fire Service. This view shows the Edwardian Garden designed by Sir Edwin Lutyens and planted by Gertrude Jekyll.

Opposite page:
A monastery in ruins

The village of Washford was the home of Cleeve Abbey – a Cistercian monastery now in ruins and cared for by English Heritage.

Immovable object

Not the real 'Excalibur' but a lifelike replica of the 'sword in the stone' on display outside the Somerset County Museum in Taunton Castle.

Opposite page:
Ruins on the Levels

The ruins of a Saxon, then Benedictine Abbey can be found at Muchelney which was, in its time, the second largest in Somerset after Glastonbury.

Medieval larder

The Abbot's Fish House, at Meare is an ancient building in which the abbots of Glastonbury Abbey used to store their fish, caught locally in the once massive – but now drained – Meare Pool.

Opposite page:
Close confinement

This unique 1779 lock-up is where Castle Cary's criminals cooled their heels. It is only 7ft in diameter and must have been quite cramped with more than about 3 felons!

Instantly recognisable landmark
If there's one landmark that says 'Somerset' it's this – Glastonbury Tor
with its fifteenth-century tower of St Michael on the summit.

Harvest under the Tor

Close to, the Tor is an impressive sight, and the views from the top are panoramic. It is now in the care of the National Trust who look after the upkeep of its footpaths and St Michael's tower.

King Arthur's resting place?

The ruins of Glastonbury's once magnificent Abbey contain a site discovered by the monks in 1191 which they claimed to be King Arthur's tomb. The only complete building in the entire Abbey site is the Abbot's Kitchen where 4 ovens were kept busy feeding the considerable number of inhabitants.

Harnessing the wind
There are a couple of notable windmills in Somerset; England's last thatched windmill is
Stembridge Tower Mill at High Ham and is now the property of the National Trust.
Ashton windmill is a restored eighteenth-century flour mill that last worked in 1927.

Holiday cottage – castle attached
Only a few of the walls of Stogursey Castle still stand, but its gatehouse – complete
with drawbridge – is a tastefully restored thatched holiday cottage let.

Liquid harvest
This is a cider apple – it looks just like an eating apple, but it tastes awful – until it's turned into cider.

Opposite page:
Orchard above the Levels
The blossom on these apple trees overlooking the Levels near Moorlynch will soon fall to leave behind the crop that more people associate with Somerset than any other – cider apples.

Peat beehives

This is the most valuable commodity on the Somerset Levels – peat – which is extracted and left to dry in these interestingly shaped 'beehives' before being sold to the horticultural industry.

Brymore frost
A weak sun melts the frost in the grounds of Brymore school – a state school
with a curriculum that specialises in agriculture, horticulture and technology.

Summer wheatfield
The end of the harvest in a field near Kingsdon – and the end of this book.